Don't be fooled by the format and delightful illustrations into thinking this is just a frivolous book. The definitions have the substance to really make a difference in people's lives. It is fun to read but it is also a serious resource to help struggling couples.

Bill O'Hanlon,
Author, *Love is a Verb* and *Rewriting Love Stories*

At last, the perfect wedding and anniversary gift! Taking to heart the principles of *Why Don't You Understand? A Gender Relationship Dictionary* could set new couples on the right track and keep established ones from careening off the rails. So if you're serious about improving communication and reducing hostilities with your Other, there's no better place to start than with this lexicon of gender-specific language.

Bonnie Casey
Author, *Growing in Circles: My Struggle to Make Peace with God, Myself, and Just About Everything*

Every day could be Valentine's Day with a book like this in your back pocket!

Prill Boyle
Author, *Defying Gravity: A Celebration of Late-Blooming Women*

More than a dictionary, this is a wonderfully organized **encyclopedia,** rich in cross references. Each entry is a crisp description of a particular problem…and … deepens the good conversation that is at the heart of a couple's relationship. This is a truly engaging book, easy to use and and difficult to forget. It will find a cherished place in my office library, and will be a pre-scribed "medication" for many of my patients

> **Don-David Lusterman, Ph.D.**
> Author, *Infidelity: A Survival Guide*

This dictionary teaches couples the ultimate goal of reducing miscommunication, hurt, and conflict. The definitions are user friendly and easy to understand. Lewis' suggestions are simple to implement, the car-toon illustrations are fun and creative. This book should be on every couple's bedside table and on every marital therapist's book shelf.

> **Beth Erickson, Ph.D.**
> Author, *Marriage Isn't for Sissies: 7 Simple Keys to Unlocking The Best Part of Your Life*

As a family mediator, I observe the male/female dynamic in its most destructive forms. Often, neither client hears the statement in the same way I do because of the emotion or need for facts and supporting data. Dr. Karen Gail Lewis offers a guide that I can put into the hands of couples (married or divorced) who can learn to hear and respond in a manner that will allow each to get their needs met. This "dictionary" will prove to be an invaluable resource.

Marie Hill, LPCC
Mediator/Counselor

Imagine having someone explain what you mean when you're talking, taking the time to define words you thought you knew, but didn't really. Someone smart, who has listened to thousands of couples trying to talk, who was clever enough to realize that what they needed was a dictionary, real explanations of what the words they're saying actually meant. Thank goodness, Dr. Karen Gail Lewis has defined what our words really mean.

Esther Cohen
Author, *Don't Mind Me (and other Jewish lies)*

Too many couples unintentionally hurt each other. Their efforts at being loving or helpful are misunderstood; they feel unappreciated, ignored or rebuffed. This dictionary will not only explain why this happens, but it will also show how to communicate in their partner's language.

Orland W.Wooley, Ph.D.
Author, *Magnolia Park, 1957*

This tremendously useful book gives couples the definition and the solution to common (and often dead-end) gender-bender misunderstandings from **A**dvice to **W**inner/Loser arguments, and everything in-between. I think every couple could benefit from reading this book.

B. Janet Hibbs, Ph.D.
Author, *Try to See It My Way: Being Fair in Love and Marriage*

Inappropriate or insufficient communication regarding money matters has helped sink many a marriage. The communication tools in *Why Don't You Understand?* provide a lifeboat – possibly to rescue the marriage and certainly for smoother sailing into the future!

Amy Whitlatch *CFP(R), CDFA(TM)*
Divorce Financial Planning Specialist

Many singles have problems in finding a good partner. One reason may be their way of communicating is not understood or appreciated by the opposite sex. This dictionary will translate these differences and show how to express their loving and angry feelings in the other's language style.

Lydia Lambert, Ph.D.
Author, *Kissing Frogs: The Path to A Prince*

If you've ever engaged in Martian-speak while the other is speaking Venus-ese, you'll want to grab a copy of this reference guide. It will help you manage expectations properly, thereby enriching your relationships and the time you spend on them. It's a must-have for any couple whose communication falters beyond 'Pass the salt.'

Christine Louise Hohlbaum
Author, *The Power of Slow: 101 Ways to Save Time in Our 24/7 World*

This is an excellent sourcebook to help individuals better understand how men and women use language. It provides excellent insight into differences, and the dictionary-style makes it easy to use. Good communication is a vital part of a relationship. whether a couple is married, or divorced and raising children together. This is a helpful, thoughtful guidebook on relationships and communication.

Sherri Goren Slovin,
Collaborative Divorce Lawyer

Why Don't You Understand is exactly right. The shoes a person chooses to wear reveals their entire life story. That's why trying on your lover's shoes (figuratively) is one of the quickest ways to understand them better. Instantly, we can see the world from their perspective.

Donna Sozio
Shoe-ologist, dating expert, and author, *Never Trust a Man in Alligator Loafers: What his Shoes Really Say About his True Love Potential*

This book is refreshing! It is written in such a clear, easy-to-understand manner about the gender differences in the way we speak to each other. I thoroughly enjoyed it and I highly recommend it to others - whether you are married or not."

Carol Ann Wilson, *CFP, CFDP*
Certified Financial Divorce Practitioner

The number one cause of failure in any form of relationship is a break down in communication. Lewis deftly and intelligently shows men and women how to become fluent in both female-ese and male-ese, enabling them to use their new-found bilingual skills to the betterment of every type of relationship they encounter. The book is at once entertaining, fun, informative, and thought-provoking. I highly recommend it as a must-read dictionary. Webster must be rolling in his grave!

Ron Stout, M.S.
Author, *Secrets From Inside The Clubhouse: What Men REALLY Think About Women*

WHY DON'T YOU UNDERSTAND?

A GENDER RELATIONSHIP DICTIONARY

Dr. Karen Gail Lewis

From this

to this

Illustrations by Brian Hagen, 2009. Please visit more of his art at
www.brian-hagen.com.

First published by Dog Ear Publishing
4010 W. 86th Street, Ste H
Indianapolis, IN 46268
www.dogearpublishing.net

ISBN: 978-160844-025-2

This book is printed on acid-free paper.

Printed in the United States of America

To the important women in my life: my mother, my four nieces, my best friend Beth, and all the female clients who have trusted their stories and lives to me over the decades,

To the important men in my life: my father, my brothers Doug and Steve, my old lovers, and all the male clients, especially my men's therapy groups, who have taught me about men. Because of you, I learned what Male-ese was before I ever had a name for it.

And to Steve, for the practice I get every day communicating in Male-ese and Female-ese.

.

ACKNOWLEDGMENTS

This dictionary could not have happened without the work of those who have come before me, laying the groundwork. I am indebted to Deborah Tannen's scholarly research on gender communication and her ability to write about it for the general public in *You Just Don't Understand: Men and Women in Conversation.*

Thanks to John Gray who made the words Mars and Venus household names with his *Men Are from Mars, Women Are from Venus: The Classic Guide to Understanding the Opposite Sex.*

This book also could not have happened without my dear friend and editor, Cindy Barrilleaux. You are always there for me, pushing and prodding, and making me a better writer. Thanks from the bottom of my *Synonym Finder.*

My big thanks to Rena Tobey: you were always ready with brilliant ideas for whatever problem I encountered.

I am also appreciative of the men and women who read sections of this dictionary, giving me feedback, and voting on the title. Alphabetically, they are Jill Applegate, Connie Fox, Tom Kalin, my niece Ami Lynn Lewis, my un-nephew Tom Miller, Grace Newman. Gary Schneider, Les Swift, Mary Snow, and Wayne (Stonewall) Wooley, And, to a man named John whom I met on a plane, thanks for your feedback on the title. I offer my sincere apologies to anyone I have inadvertently overlooked.

TABLE OF CONTENTS

INTRODUCTION

When I was 20 years old, I lived in London for a month. One day, while waiting for a bus, I struck up a conversation with a man and his young daughter. He said he was taking her to get her fringe cut. I was puzzled, and asked if the fringe was on a dress or a blouse. They laughed so loudly that passersby turned and looked. The little girl giggled. "Fringe is what you Americans call bangs."

When traveling in a foreign country, we don't expect to understand the language. But in an English speaking country, we assume we speak the same language. In the same way, men and women share the same language and assume they will understand one another. But it just isn't true.

After almost four decades as a marriage and family therapist, I have concluded that over 60% of marital problems result from misunderstandings men and women don't even know they are having — misunderstandings based on differences in gender communication and expectations. (And that percentage goes even higher if one or both of the couple have Attention Deficit Disorder.) Perhaps men and women don't speak the same language after all.

Why a gender dictionary?

To some extent, men and women do have their separate languages; men speak Male-ese and women speak Female-ese. One language is not better than the other; there is no right or wrong. Problems occur, though, when couples are not clear about their language differences. They assume their gendered way of speaking is the "right" way, and are annoyed when their partner doesn't "get it." When this happens, the miscommunication can be painful, if not fatal, to their relationship.

I decided to create this dictionary to help both men and women learn the words and behaviors of their own *and each other's* gender. I've seen over and over again, when couples become fluent in both Male-ese and Female-ese, they can achieve greater contentment and a more solid relationship. Without this understanding, they may easily become offended by what the other person, perhaps innocently, says or does. Therefore, this dictionary can help by translating the differences. Miscommunication *is* avoidable.

Who is this dictionary for?

This dictionary is designed for heterosexual married and single men and women in intimate relationships, as well as singles who are getting to know a potential mate.

It also is helpful for adult siblings, especially as you try to make joint decisions about your aging parents, but may end up not speaking to each other. Understanding Male-ese and Female-ese helps translate intractable and hateful arguments that become personal attacks into successful communication.

It may also be beneficial to gay and lesbian couples, as well as close friends, where the two people involved have had a misunderstanding, or are pursuing incompatible communication strategies. While it is aimed at communication between people in a close personal relationship, many of the same concepts are applicable at work and in any male-female relationships.

What is in the dictionary?

This book is divided into five parts: It starts with The Prologue that gives three sample conversations between couples that went awry because the men and women did not understand Male-ese and Female-ese.

The Dictionary itself defines and gives examples of more than 70 specific words and phrases, with cross-referencing where appropriate.

The Epilogue repeats the three exchanges from the Prologue, noting specific gender words that led to each argument. Each exchange is then repeated again, demonstrating how the conversation might have been handled differently if both partners were respectful of the Male-ese and Female-ese differences. The Epilogue also contains a longer illustration of a good argument, highlighting specific words and terms that make it bilingual.

The Appendix provides four tips and solutions for enhancing a good, gender-sensitive conversation.

The book concludes with Your Personal Inventory List which is where you track the words and terms that cause problems within your relationship. This can become your individual resource guide for helping you become bilingual and for maneuvering through conversations with your partner without getting stuck in arguments.

How can you use this dictionary?

As with all dictionaries, the words and terms here are arranged alphabetically and include cross referencing. With a standard dictionary, though, when you are stuck about the meaning of a word, you look it up. But, when couples get stuck in a misunderstanding or conflict, they are not aware of the cause, so there is no word or term to look up.

Therefore, to get the best mileage out of this dictionary read it straight through. Become familiar with the terms. Do this alone or with your partner. As you are reading, each of you use a different color to highlight the terms that seem familiar to your communication difficulties or that are emotionally charged.

Then turn to Your Personal Inventory List. This has all the words in the dictionary. Check the words you each have highlighted. At a quiet time, you and your partner can discuss the terms you marked and reread the descriptions. You can also reread the Good Argument in the Epilogue and the examples in the Appendix for ideas about how to *replay* your part of an argument.

When you are not in the midst of an argument practice what you learn from the examples. Then, after an argument, go back to the terms you have checked and see where you got tripped up; think how you could handle the same situation differently the next time it arises.

The dictionary can continue to be an on-going resource for whenever a conversation or argument is not going well.

It is helpful if your partner does this with you, but as you will learn in the Epilogue- Couples 2 and 3, when one person changes, there is often reactive change in the other.

Final thoughts

As you read through the descriptions of the words and phrases in this dictionary, you will chuckle with recognition and exclaim "Ah Ha," as you gain insight into why some conversations turn bad. However, you will, of course, also find some descriptions that do not fit you at all, or not all the time.

Women may think these ideas are old fashioned, "We are no longer like that." It is true, women have changed in many ways, in fact, they have adapted many traits of Male-ese. (See my article, "Henry Higgins You Got Your Wish - Unfortunately" at http://www.DrKGL.com/HH.) But, there are often lingering traits you assume are just part of who you are when, in fact, they are part of Female-ese.

Men may think there is no male mandate to "be a winner not a loser." Yet, behaviors that women see as unthoughtful, when understood in context to the historical mandate, take on a different meaning. So, even if the descriptions seem exaggerated or don't fit, don't discount them too quickly. Sometimes an exaggeration makes it easier to see what is causing the miscommunication.

For some couples the gender roles are reversed. Note, though, if they are always reversed or if only in some situations. As you and your partner discuss your highlighted terms, think about whether the times you get tripped up are when you are talking in Male-ese and Female-ese.

PROLOGUE

To understand why a Gender Dictionary is necessary, read the excerpts from three different conversations below. All three conversations are between couples who love each other. They may sound similar to conversations you have had with a partner.

The first couple is arguing after returning from a party. The second couple is arguing about flowers the man has given the woman. And the third couple is discussing which movie to rent.

In the Epilogue, you will see these same three conversations repeated with explanations, based on the dictionary words, of what each was doing that contributed to the argument. The Epilogue also shows how the same conversations could have been handled differently if both partners were aware of the gender languages of Male-ese and Female-ese.

Couple 1: After the Party

"Ok. What's up?" he sighs. "You've been quiet ever since we left home this evening. I thought it was a great party, but you've been pouty."

"I'm not pouty," she pouts.

"Come off it, of course you are. Something's been bothering you from the moment we got in the car."

"No, from the moment I came down the stairs and you didn't say a thing about how I looked." She tears up.

"Huh? Is that what this is about? Is that why you didn't speak to me the whole drive over and looked so hurt all evening?" He's exasperated. "You looked lovely; you always do. I'm always proud of how you look."

"You didn't tell me." Against her best intentions, there is a slight whine.

"You didn't ask."

"You should tell me without my having to ask." The whine is stronger now. "Otherwise, I don't know if you are just saying it because I asked."

Couple 2: The Flowers

They sit in my office glaring at each other. He finally turns to her and growls, "I can never do enough for you! It's one complaint after another. I know women like flowers, so I send you roses, but even that wasn't right. You never even put them in a vase. After a while, I just gave up."

"I didn't say anything the first two times you brought me flowers because I thought it was romantic, and I didn't want to hurt your feelings. But the third time, I reminded you I'm allergic to them. You never listened to me and kept giving them to me for Valentine's Day, or just as an "I love you" surprise. So, I'd just put them aside. The flowers just became another example of how you never listen to me."

Couple 3: The Movies

One overcast Sunday afternoon, she asks, "What movie should we rent tonight?"

He, glued to the TV, says, "How about *King Kong*?"

Silence.

"I've never seen any of the Humphrey Bogart movies," she offers.

Not taking his eyes from the football game, he nods. "That's fine; whatever you want."

"You never listen to me!" she snaps.

He jerks his head up, now looking directly at her. First surprise, then anger flashes in his eyes. "Oh, for chrissake! What's the big deal? You didn't listen to me about buying that new blender. I couldn't care less which movie we see. In fact, I don't care if we see one or not!" As he storms out of the room, he shouts, "You're never satisfied! You always have to pick on me."

~~~~~~~~~~~

Line up 10 men behind the men in these stories, and at least 9 will be nodding their heads in recognition. They understand exactly how the man was feeling in each of these situations.

Line up 10 women behind the women in these stories, and at least 9 will be nodding their heads in recognition. They understand exactly how the woman was feeling in each of these situations.

In the Epilogue, we return to these three couples noting the Male-ese and Female-ese terms they used, how they could have handled the situation differently.

DICTIONARY

Advice

Men express their affection and let their partners know they love and care for them by being helpful (see I Love You). This shows up primarily in giving advice and suggestions about how to do things or resolve problems.

Women, however, do not perceive unsolicited suggestions as a sign of love. When a man offers this gift, the woman may think he is telling her what to do (see Pleasing the Other). She may feel like a child with her father, or that he is belittling her, assuming she can't figure out what to do on her own. Thus, his caring comes across as condescension.

These days, most men know women don't like unsolicited advice, yet they continue to offer it. (See my article, "Men: You Know Better, But…," at http://www. DrKGL.com/MenKnow.) This is because in Male-ese, not to do so would mean they are being unloving and unkind.

Instead of giving unsolicited advice to express caring, there are two things men can do for women that will be appreciated. One, they can listen. (Yes, men, that *is* doing something.) And two, after listening, they can ask, "Would you like a suggestion?" The asking, rather than just giving, allows the woman to make the choice as to whether she wants a suggestion or not, and if she does, whether she wants it now or later. It also gives her the chance to say no, she just wanted to know the man was listening (see Epilogue- Men: An Alternative to Giving Advice).

Even if she turns down his offer of advice, she will appreciate his effort, and he will have the satisfaction of having offered his help. That will make it easier for him to say nothing else.

Affairs

Anyone can have an affair. They usually start insidiously, sneaking up on a person. However, the temperature of the couple's relationship environment must be real cool for an affair to blossom.

An affair is defined here as one member of a couple investing emotional energy and time in something or someone in lieu of, not in addition to, the spouse. Contrary to popular thought, affairs do not have to involve sex or love.

Many couples begin their first non-sexual affairs – with the children, work, alcohol, golf, tennis — when the excitement of romance fades and everyday life takes more investment. (See my article, "Are You Having an Affair? Do You Even Know?" at http://www.DrKGL.com/affairs.)

At some point, one or both partners will long for more connection than the daily routine. It's the challenge of long-term marriages. However, if the bond between the couple is weak or non-existent, there will be space for another person to move in and fill the emotional void. Thus begins a sexual affair.

Anger

The word anger is commonly used to mean both the emotional feeling of anger and the action you take when feeling angry. Yet, the feeling comes first; then

comes the discussion if or whether to take action.

Feelings: If you are human, you feel anger. It is an emotion, just like happiness or sadness. You can't control its arrival. It is impossible *not* to feel the emotion of anger.

Most people confuse the feeling of anger with the action. They are hesitant to acknowledge when they feel anger because they don't want to take action. Moreover, they think any behavior in response to anger must be negative (see Epilogue- Good Argument).

Actions: The action that results from anger can be anything from one extreme of being violent to the other extreme of denying your feelings. Many people teach themselves not to notice the physical feelings associated with anger. If they don't acknowledge the anger, they think they won't have to take action. Not enough people have learned that the best action is to *express the feeling*.

Many couples avoid noticing their anger so they don't have to deal with it. When this happens, one partner may be unaware how the other is feeling. Yet often this leads to the anger being expressed indirectly. Or, the anger can be expressed through sarcasm or passive aggressive behavior – where the person can act one way but deny it has anything to do with being angry at the partner. Either way, the issues underlying the anger never get resolved because it is not addressed directly.

Men and women typically deal with their feelings of anger differently. In childhood, boys often learn that anger = fighting (see Winner/Loser). Memories of this equation often prevent men from feeling their anger. Instead, they remove themselves from the situation or become moody. Ironically, because in Male-ese men are not supposed to acknowledge the softer emotions like sadness or loneliness, they may cover these feelings with anger. This causes them to remove themselves from the situation, or flee, or get cranky (see Emotional Pain, Arguments- Stress and Physiology).

Conversely, since Female-ese discourages women from feeling and expressing anger, they often transform the feeling into sadness or disappointment. For most women, these are emotions with acceptable actions: they can cry and complain (see Tears).

Apology/I'm Sorry

Men do not easily or directly apologize when they believe they have done something minor or seriously wrong, such as hurting their partner's feelings, or worrying her, or forgetting to pick up the clothes at the dry cleaner. Having to say, "I'm sorry," is a public acknowledgement of their mistake, which may activate their shame and humiliation (see Shame).

Men are socialized from early childhood to be winners. If they are not, the only alternative is to be a loser, which no male would willingly choose (see Winner/Loser). When a man says, "I'm sorry," he is admitting he has done something un-winner-like – that is, he is a loser.

Women are socialized so differently that they don't understand this. They say "I'm sorry" whenever things don't go well, even if it's clearly not their fault. Research has shown that with something as simple as someone stepping on a woman's foot, she is likely to do the apologizing. It does not mean she thinks she has done something wrong; it means "I'm sorry things didn't go well." (Or in the case of being stepped on, "I'm sorry you are in the position of feeling bad for having stepped on my foot.")

In addition, women sometimes even help a man not apologize by making excuses for him. If a man broke something or forgot the dry cleaning, women may say, "No problem," "Don't worry about it," or "It's not a big deal," whether it's a big deal or not (see I'm Fine). This may be related to their concern about not making the man feel bad (see Fragile Ego).

Arguments

Arguments are far more complex than just men and women exchanging angry words. There are several components that play into the difficulties involved in arguing.

Meaning: Arguments have different meanings for men and women. For men, an argument is a debate to be won or lost. And since being a loser is the worst damage to a man's self-esteem, men may argue their hardest, whether the fight is about who paid the electric bill last month or the quality of a local restaurant (see Winner/Loser).

Women are socialized to get along, to compromise, to not stand above others. Therefore, a woman's goal in an argument is to be heard and to find a compromise or a win/win solution. The man, however, within his framework, may see her as trying to win, to one-up him, so he may fight back harder. Without understanding the different meanings men and women give to arguing, couples are having two different encounters.

Verbal Encounter: For women, a verbal encounter is an exchange of ideas in which they want to express their thoughts and hear what the man has to say (see Conversation- Purpose). For women, the final outcome (who is right or wrong), while important, is less crucial than feeling the man has really heard what they have to say.

Often, men experience these encounters as the woman asking for their opinion, so they give it (see Conversation- Purpose). Or, they interpret the encounter as her wanting knowledge or advice, so they give it (see Advice). Or, they may think she is arguing, or questioning their comments, so they argue their point.

Without understanding these differences, a verbal encounter can be like men and women on the same playing field, but one has a polo stick and the other a softball.

Stress and Physiology: Because men and women have different physiological make ups, the stress of arguments has different effects. Men's stress levels get acti-

vated significantly sooner than do women's. So, when arguing, men experience far more emotional stress than women. When they feel attacked (even verbally), men's internal fight or flight signals are triggered (see Anger-Actions, Winner/Loser).

A fighting reaction does not necessarily mean a physical attack. But in a verbal argument, men often counterattack with forcefulness as if they had been physically attacked. Therefore, to keep the one-up status of a winner, they may shift the topic so they can blame the woman for something; that way, they can be back on top (see Arguments- Deflect The Conversation, Arguments-Tit for Tat, Blame).

Sometimes, instead of fighting back, men flee from an argument; they may silently (or noisily) leave the room. Other possibilities include their emotionally removing themselves, by becoming engrossed in television, the computer, or the newspaper, or just falling asleep (see Anger- Actions).

Women can engage in an argument a lot longer than men because, as research now suggests, physiologically their bodies do not react as quickly to stress. While both men and women want the other to hear what they have to say, women often are more invested in being heard than the end result.

Dirty Fighting: This is an indirect means of arguing used by both men and women. People resort to dirty fighting when they are uncomfortable handling their negative feelings. Rather than expressing their anger in a polite and direct manner, they do it in an underhanded, backhanded, or sneaky way.

One example of dirty fighting is sarcasm. Another is passively accepting what the other has said or done, and then later getting back at that person. Dirty fighting can also include bringing up unrelated issues during an argument, saying something intentionally to hurt the other person. A less obvious form of dirty fighting is pretending everything is fine (see I'm Fine).

Since all couples have disagreements, those who proudly say they never argue probably express their unresolved feelings through an indirect means of dirty fighting.

Tit for Tat: Criticism or a complaint can be given and received politely. But when it is not, the receiver may defensively respond with tit for tat. In this maneuver, one partner's complaint about the other is met with a counter-complaint. For example, if a woman reminds the man he forgot to turn off the kitchen light, he immediately counters with, "You forgot last week." Another possibility is that the man counters with something entirely different, such as "You never remember to get the oil changed in your car." The purpose of a tit for tat is to deflect blame (see Blame, Arguments- Deflect the Conversation).

Sometimes, highly-shamed men can interpret a neutral comment as a criticism, or a sign of having failed, and respond with a tit for tat (see Shame, Winner/Loser).

While women do a tit for tat to avoid feeling blamed, their defensiveness may also come from feeling they have let the man down. Alternatively, they may feel the need to defend themselves from feeling powerless with him.

Deflect the Conversation: (see Blame, Arguments- Tit for Tat). When a man or woman feels defensive in a conversation, deflecting the topic is an avoidance maneuver. While similar to externalizing and tit for tat, deflecting just changes the topic or the direction of the topic.

For instance, she says, "You forgot to buy crackers," and he replies, "You didn't write it on the list." If she says, "You eat them more than I do," this can lead to an argument about who actually eats more of the crackers. The original topic, the forgotten crackers, are now forgotten.

Good Argument: A good argument occurs when both the man and the woman stick to the topic, feel their points have been heard, and come to a resolution in which neither feels like the loser.

Understanding the gender differences in arguing, including the purpose of arguing and the physiological make up of men and women, and the avoidance of tit for tats provide the basic tools for a good argument. (For an example of how these terms and others in the dictionary can be used to have a good argument, see Epilogue.)

Here is a technique to ensure couples hear what each other says. After one person makes a statement or complaint, the other person repeats it, beginning with, "I hear you say that…" If the person being spoken to does not accurately repeat what was said or intended, the speaker tries to make the point clearer. If both people do this for each point, it assures they will both feel heard and understood.

Too many times couples engage in unresolvable arguments simply because they are not even arguing about the same issue: they haven't really heard what the other is saying.

The closeness that results from a good argument can be so powerful, it is not surprising some couples end up making love. It's as if the intensity of the emotional closeness leads to an intense sexual explosion.

Blame

How men and women deal with blame is often gender based. Research shows men tend to externalize the blame, laying fault on the woman while women tend to blame themselves.

Externalize: To externalize means seeing the events as outside of one's control. This is more typical within Male-ese. A man is likely to blame someone or some thing for what has happened rather than own his part in causing the situation. This can be around minor events, like blaming the bowl for being in the way when he knocked it over. Or, it can be around more serious events like blaming the woman for causing whatever the problem. While he may feel bad, or even shame, for breaking a bowl or hurting the woman's feelings, he may not verbalize his responsibililty (see Shame, Winner/Loser).

Internalize: To internalize means accepting personal control over the events of one's life. This is more typical within Female-ese. Women look within themselves for what they could or should have done differently. Often they twist their internalizing into beating themselves up with self-blame (see Blame- Self-Blame).

Self-Blame: Women have been socialized to internalize. From childhood on, they have absorbed the message it is their job to prevent relationship problems. Therefore, if there is a problem, it must be their fault (see Cultural Roles, Identity).

Single women in particular have absorbed the societal message that not having a man is their fault. So they think that if they can identify a flaw in themselves that is causing them to be single, they can fix that problem, and – so goes the Female-ese reasoning – they will be able to find a man. This Fix-It Solution gives them a sense of control. Without it, they are left with no control over or explanation for why they have not met an appropriate man. (See my article, "For Single Women: The Fix-It Solution," at http://www.DrKGL.com/fixit.)

Personalize: A man can make a statement or do something that may have nothing to do with a woman, but because women internalize blame, they personalize it, assuming there is some meaning for them. If the man is upset about something, she must figure out what she did wrong and then fix the problem (see Blame- Externalize/Internalize, Cultural Roles, QTIP).

Given this reasoning, women are always on the alert for hidden meanings. "What did he mean when he said he didn't enjoy his breakfast? Was he mad at me because I didn't make him eggs today? Should I have bought a different kind of cereal?" That he may have an upset stomach never occurred to her. Usually men have no idea women do this.

Personalizing leads to ongoing self-doubt and self-questioning. And it fits nicely with men's tendency to externalize. Thus, when there is a problem, a man blames the woman and she blames herself. Ironically, they both agree it is her fault.

Change Yourself, Not Your Partner

When one partner is bothered by something the other does, the tendency is to expect the other to change. One of the hardest things to accept is the impossibility of changing another person. One may think making a complaint will produce a change, but it does not (see Relationship Expectations).

Partners can tell each other what they like or don't like, or what adjustments they want. Then, it's up to each of them to decide whether or not to make the change. If several good arguments/discussions have not resulted in change, *stop*. The definition of stupid is to keep doing the same thing and hoping to get a different result. The old adage, "If at first you don't succeed, try, try again," is not true in relationships. (See my article, "Three Steps to Stop Kvetching About Men," at http://www.DrKGL.com/kvetch.)

To produce change, people must change themselves. The only control they have is to question what they can do that will make the situation better. That's all. And according to physics, for every action there is an equal or opposite reaction. There cannot be *no* reaction. So changing the self may result in some reverberating change in the other. But even if not, the one who wants and makes the change can feel proud at having taken control by handling their part of the situation (see Arguments- Good Argument, Epilogue, and Relationship Expectations).

Communication Style

Differences in communication style have been well popularized in recent years. However, it's important to understand these styles in some detail in order to be clear when a misunderstanding is occurring because a couple is not bilingual. While there are many books written about gender differences, here are some concepts that are rarely considered, and which underscore the nuances of Male-ese and Female-ese.

Verbal Tennis: Women's conversational style is like Verbal Tennis. One hits a topic over the net, and the other hits it back. The couple stays on that topic until one hits a new topic across court, and the other person responds to the new topic.

What each one says is a response to, an example of, or a story based on the other person's comments.

This can cause problems because in Male-ese, there is no obligation to respond with the same topic. Men hear a woman speak and assume she stops when she has finished with what she wants to say (see Conversation- Purpose). So the man feels he is free to start another topic. He does not understand that in Female-ese, women expect a back-and-forth flow of conversation on one topic before moving to another.

Sharing Ideas: In important conversations, men want to have their ideas shaped and well formulated before speaking. To do otherwise risks their sounding vague, that is, sounding like a loser (see Winner/Loser). This is very different for women, who often clarify their ideas while speaking. Men may describe women's style as verbal meandering, and they'd be right. Often women hear what they are saying while speaking, adjusting their comments as they go along.

Therefore, it is usually wise for a man to not assume that the woman means every sentence she says. A man should wait until she is finished, until she has arrived at the point she wants to make.

Sharing Feelings: Men and women are famously different in regard to sharing feelings. Men generally are uncomfortable, while this is a strong suit for women.

Men often feel vulnerable in sharing their personal feelings. And, that vulnerability makes them feel weak, less manly (see Winner/Loser). They are not usually skilled in being closely in touch with what they feel, so expressing it – even when they want to – does not flow easily.

Men have an array of techniques for avoiding personal conversations. They may start an argument with a woman to abort any closeness. They may withdraw, physically or emotionally, falling asleep in the middle of a woman's sharing, or turning to the newspaper or computer.

For women, sharing personal feelings is a pleasure and a sign of closeness (see Conversation- Purpose). They want to tell men stories or experiences that have meaning for them. And they feel close to a man when he can expose his feelings and vulnerabilities. For women, this is a turn-on, the best aphrodisiac (see Sex- Female Aphrodisiac, and Sex- Pre-Foreplay).

Direct/Indirect: Men usually express their concerns and preferences in a direct, definitive manner. They like something, they want something, they say it.

Women express their concerns or preferences indirectly. It may come out as a question. Rather than saying, "I want steak for dinner; how about you?" they might say, "Would you like steak for dinner?" Instead of, "I'm hot so I'm turning on the air conditioner," they ask, "Are you hot?"

Put this together with how men do conversations (see Conversation- Questions), and a man will hear the question about steak (or temperature) and answer yes or no. He may not ask her in return what she would like (see Communication Style- Verbal Tennis). This can leave the woman feeling as if he doesn't care what she wants. And that can lead to her feeling he doesn't care about her (see Blame-Personalize).

Another way women are indirect includes asking one question but really meaning something entirely different. For instance, "How do I look?" might translate to "Do you love me?" This is not a conscious maneuver; women rarely know they are doing it. The trick for men is to be alert to the woman's "question behind the question" (see Miscommunication-Question behind the Question.)

Being indirect is also a problem between women – even though both speak Female-ese. Often friendships develop problems or end because the women were not clear enough about their issues – they either never spoke up or did so indirectly.

Listening: Women and men have very different styles of listening. Men's ability to listen closely may be heightened by not looking at the person to whom they are speaking. Looking at the other person may distract them from hearing what is being said. Men listen quietly, without giving verbal or nonverbal indications they have heard the other. It is enough for them to listen. They assume you know they are listening. When talking with other men, they trust they are being listened to, even if the conversation is interspersed with a discussion of sports or car repairs.

Women not only need to see the person to whom they are talking, they give verbal and non-verbal indications they are listening. Without receiving those indications, they do not feel they are being heard.

If unaware of these gender differences, men and women assume the other listens in their own gender style. This can cause anger and disappointment without the couple realizing why

Voice Level: Men's voices are usually deeper than women's. So, when they get anxious or stressed, as in an emotional discussion or argument, their voices get even deeper or louder. It's an indication they feel frustrated or worried or even scared, but women often hear the raised voice as shouting and may feel threatened. Women, especially those raised by a loud or cruel father, may overreact to a loud voice.

Here's an example of how voice level differences can lead to a misunderstanding. In an argument, if the man feels his point is not being heard, out of frustration, he raises his voice. The woman tells him to stop yelling. This increases his frustration, so he yells louder. Which reinforces her comlaint that he is yelling. This cycle can keep escalating with neither of them feeling understood.

Competition

In competitive situations, in a game, work, even cooking or mowing the lawn, both men and women may want to win. But the intent behind the competition may be different for men than for women.

For men, competition arises from the messages they have received about being a man, about winning. They are socialized with the Winner/Loser mandate, so they strive to make sure they are not the loser. And if they are not to be the loser, that automatically means the woman has to be. Often, men do not care about making a woman lose, they are only focused on making sure they are the winner (see Identity, Winner/Loser).

For women, competition often comes from a different internal place. Their gender message says they should not stand out or be better than the man (see Identity). Since culturally they are taught men are fragile, they shouldn't outshine a man (see Identity, Fragile Ego). When women are angry that the man always has to win, they may fight back hard. The competition, though, comes more from the battle for control or righting a power imbalance with the man than from a sense of "I must win" (see Control).

Compliments

While this issue is not entirely gender-specific, women need compliments more often than men (see Relationship Expectations- Shoebox and Mantel). For women, a compliment means the man is paying attention to them, appreciates them, values them.

Yet, they often rebuff a compliment with a self-effacing comment. For instance, if a man says how well a woman sings, she is likely to say, "No, I am not really good," or, "You should hear my sister sing" (see Thank You). Or the man says something complimentary and the woman says, "You're only saying that because you know I want to hear it."

Men may like receiving a compliment, but they may feel it is unmanly to show they need it. And, if they do not get a compliment, may are less likely to personalize it (see QTIP).

Control

It is not uncommon for couples to get into control battles, each one wanting to win, to be right, to have the other recognize his or her correctness. They may argue over serious issues, but too often they argue over issues as mundane as who is right about the best route to a restaurant, where they bought a painting, or whose memory of a recent conversation is more accurate.

For women, though, the battle for control may also have another layer of meaning besides just winning. Their need to have control over a man may stem from their feeling less powerful in society and/or in their family because they are female.

I'm Right: For many couples, the issue involved in an argument is consistently less important than proving themselves right and their partner wrong. The topic of the discussion or argument

is *not* the issue. It is important for both people to figure out which is more important for them – being right or proving the other wrong. These are two separate issues (see Miscommunication). (See my article, "You're Both 100% Right!" at http://www.drkgl.com/100.)

When couples get caught in an "I'm Right" battle, they have lost sight of their being on the same team. They have moved from a loving partnership working together to adversaries who want to best the other. When this occurs, the topic is usually less important than the battle.

Here is one way to avoid the power struggle when you are arguing over what you said versus what your partner heard. Instead of repeating, "That's not what I said," you can say, "I can't guarantee what left my mouth, but I know what left my brain was...." Instead of challenging, "You didn't say that," you could offer, "I don't know what left your brain, but what got into my ears was ...."

Here is another cute way to bypass a power struggle. Keep a piece of paper on the refrigerator with a vertical line down the middle. Write one name on the top of each column. Draw straws as to who goes first. Then, every time you catch yourselves disagreeing over who is right, alternate who gets to be the winner. That way, you take turns. This method is only useful when the topic is not of serious consequence.

Conversation

It is in couples' conversations that the differences between Male-ese and Female-ese are most pronounced. Men and women have different rules – starting with the very purpose of talking.

Purpose: For men, the purpose of conversation is to report information, not to chit-chat. If asked a question, they answer it. There is no back-and-forth exchange about the topic (see Communication Style- Verbal Tennis).

When men do talk at length, they are not chatting; often they are trying to be helpful, or demonstrating their knowledge. This is in keeping with men's mandate to be a winner (see Winner/Loser).

For women, the purpose of conversation often is to connect with the other person. Research shows that exchanging words, stories, and even gossip is a female means for making personal contact, for saying, "I like you," or "Will you please like me?" To be liked or connected with someone else often is more important for women than the content of their conversation.

So, when a woman asks, "Where do you want to eat?" she expects the man will then ask her opinion. That shows he wants to connect with her, that he cares about her opinion.

Men are unlikely to respond in that way. Questions are for getting information. While they need questions to know what is being asked of them, they are less likely to initiate the question which would engage them in Female-ese Verbal Tennis (see Conversation- Questions, Communication Style- Verbal Tennis). In Male-ese, the assumption is that if a woman has something to say, she'll say it. Men don't think they have to ask.

Negotiation: In business, the purpose of negotiating is to get what you want. In personal relationships, negotiation is strongly defined by gender differences.

For women, typically, negotiation needs to result in an *internal sense of equalizing,* a win/win situation. Each must leave feeling they have benefitted equally, or at least equitably. The primary exception to this is when women feel out of control, or they have less power than the man in the conversation. Then, they may fight to make the man lose.

Men often start a negotiation from the stance of needing to win. In negotiation with women, who are more adept at personal conversations, men may feel in a one-down position. If so, they may fight harder to win. They also may feel shame for being in a loser position (see Shame, Winner/Loser).

Questions: Women ask questions for the purpose of engaging others. They may want the answer, but they want it in the context of a personal (back and forth) connection. In social settings, they have been socialized to ask a man questions to encourage him to talk about himself. Asking questions is one way to keep the verbal tennis in play (see Communication Style- Verbal Tennis).

Conversely, in personal conversations with a woman, men generally do not ask questions. They assume a woman will tell them whatever she wants them to know. While they don't ask questions, as a general rule, they wait for a question before commenting; this way they will know what the woman wants and how to respond to her (see Miscommunication).

Silence: For men, silence has many meanings. It can be an indication of closeness, for instance when fishing quietly with a male friend. Another example is sitting side by side on a porch with a friend, wordlessly watching the stars. Many men say these are some of their most intimate times.

Men are also silent when they are waiting for a question. Men are often criticized for being silent when a woman is talking to them about a relationship problem. But they are simply waiting for her to finish, waiting for her question, so they'll know how to respond (see Miscommunication Cycle, Conversation- Questions).

Another meaning of silence for men is related to shame. When flooded with anger at a woman during a conversation, men may flee from the situation – physically or emotionally. Even when they remain seated, they may disappear into their own world, shutting the woman out. By doing this, they wrap themselves in silence to quiet the internal flooding of rage or shame and to regain their composure (see   Arguments- Stress and Physiology, Shame).

The meaning of silence for a woman is very different. Women like their quiet time, but when with another person, man or woman, the need to connect is met though verbal exchanges and sharing information or feelings. Therefore, when a man is silent, the woman may feel shut out; they may assume he is upset with her, personalizing his silence (see Blame-Personalize).

Nagging: Men experience nagging as a woman repeatedly telling them what she wants them to do, like a chore. Unless intentionally ignoring the woman, men register the request, then set their own time-table for when they will get to it. If the task doesn't seem urgent to them, it goes further down their list, behind things they consider more important. If a man doesn't tell the woman what he is thinking, she believes her request is ignored, so she repeats it. Hence, the man feels nagged.

Here's what a nagging cycle between a man and woman can look like:

- She mentions something that needs to be done.
- He hears her and decides when it should be done (based on how important he feels it is, what else he has to do, how much he hates the thought of doing it, etc.).
- She sees it is not done and assumes he has forgotten or never heard her, so she reminds him again.
- He hears her again, but says nothing since he knows it's on his to-do list.
- She doesn't see it getting done, so she reminds him again.

And the cycle continues with him feeling nagged and her feeling ignored.

What happens is he does not let her know he has heard her request and he does not tell her *when* he'll complete the project. She may feel more urgency than he does in the chore being completed, but they do not discuss their different perceptions of importance. Thus, they continue the cycle, both getting angrier.

Cultural Roles

Over the centuries, men and women have been socialized along very different avenues for relating.

Men: If It Ain't Broke, Don't Fix It: There are societal messages about the attitudes that go along with being a "good" male. One of those is reflected in the adage, "If it ain't broke, don't fix it." This often turns into the typical male behavior of ignoring a relationship problem as long as possible, or until it smacks them in the face.

Men do not confront a relationship problem unless absolutely necessary because — like the boy who took apart and re-assembled a clock, only to have one piece left over — the risk is they'll make things much worse. (See my article, "If It Ain't Broke, Don't Fix It," at http://www.DrKGL.com/ain't.)

Women: Prevent Problems from Becoming Bigger: Unfortunately, one of the attitudes that make a "good" woman is exactly the opposite of the man's atti-tude in the same situation, namely "It's a woman's job to prevent a relationship problem, and if one does exists, it is her job to fix it. If you can't, it's your fault; you must not be trying hard enough."

Since women's core identity (see Identity - Core Identity) includes the belief they are responsible for important relationships, they seek out even small prob-lems to prevent them from becoming more serious. They need to fix the problem before it becomes serious and risks destroying their relationship.

Problems with Conflicting Cultural Messages: There is nothing inherently wrong with either of these messages about relationships; they just happen to be totally contradictory! Too often, a cycle occurs in which the more the woman raises concerns about a problem in the relationship, the more the man ignores it, which causes her to raise it more, and on and on. Each of them is adhering to the attitudes of their gender. To have a good relationship, men and women have to find a balance between total avoidance and total submersion in problems, when to address an issue, and how to pick the issues worthy of battle (see Appendices 2, 3, and 4).

Emotional Pain

Because of the way they are socialized, men may know when they feel anger but they may not be attuned to their softer emotions, such as sadness, loneliness, grief, rejection, They may subconsciously shift the sensation of emotional pain into physical discomfort, such as nausea or a headache. Some men sleep, eat, or drink to avoid their feelings. They may "veg out" in front of the television, or become cranky, unaware they are covering up uncomfortable feelings.

Women tend to be more in touch with their emotional pain, to recognize and talk about it. One common exception is anger. Having been raised hearing it is unfeminine to show anger, they may convert this scary feeling into sadness – a more socially acceptable feeling for women (see Anger- Feelings, Identity, Tears).

Fragile Ego

"Men have a fragile ego." Most women have been raised by their family and/or society to believe this, to view men as emotionally weak. However, this is a myth!

Women may confuse not wanting to hurt a man's feelings with his having a fragile ego. A woman may not want to hurt another woman's feelings either, but she doesn't say, "A woman has a fragile ego."

Yet, many women will let a man tell them something they already know, or win at a sport where they actually are better rather than hurt the man's ego. Or, single women may go out a second time with a man they do not like to spare his ego. This gets extrapolated to letting the man have the largest piece of cake or the last piece of chicken. If men knew they were being treated as if they were fragile, they would resent the condescension. However, this protection is so automatic, many women may not even be aware they do it.

Gift Giving

Men and women often have very different ways of giving and receiving gifts. Not understanding these differences can lead to dissatisfaction, annoyance, even anger.

Men generally prefer a woman give them a list of things she wants for her birthday, anniversary, or holiday. This way, they know she will like what they select for her. It also prevents them from choosing something she doesn't like, which might cause them to feel shame at having picked the wrong thing (see Shame, Winner/Loser). It also saves them from roaming around stores, which is something men hate.

Similarly, when it's their turn to receive a gift, they want to give the woman their list, to be assured of getting what they want.

Women, on the other hand, do not like providing a list. They think, "If I give you a list, I might as well go buy it for myself." They want the man to know them well enough to select what they would like.

Women also don't like getting a wish-list from men. If they bought off his list, there would be nothing personal in what they give him; it would not demonstrate how much thought they put into their selection. For women, selecting a special gift is a statement of caring by the giver. For men, the gift itself is the statement of caring.

The key to avoiding difficulty when giving a material gift is to give in the way the Receiver will appreciate, even if that is not what the Giver would want. So, for instance, a woman would accept a list from the man for his gift, and the man would try to think of something he knows the woman would appreciate for her gift. (See my article, "Gift Giving – Your Style or Mine?" at http://www.DrKGL.com/gift.)

Identity

Core Identity: Men's and women's core identities, what it means to be a male and a female, have been shaped by societal messages that have been passed down through generations.

For instance, a man's identity is tied up with his competence as a breadwinner and a protector of women and children. (Remember the men's orders on the

Titanic? Women and children were to be saved first.) If a man has a problem in an important relationship – with a lover, spouse, or child – he will feel horrible, worry about it, and think about how to fix the problem. Although he will feel bad, the core of his identity is not affected. He does not feel he's a failure as a male.

However, if he is not earning as much money as he feels he should to support his family, if he loses his job, or if a woman in his family is harmed, he feels like a failure as a male.

The societal message shaping women's identity is that a competent woman takes good care of her relationships. If she is having trouble at work, or if she is even fired, she will feel horrible and will question what she could have done differently. But she does not feel like a failure as a female.

However, if she is having trouble in an important relationship - partner, child, best friend, parent, or sibling - that goes directly to the core of her identify and her sense of herself, and makes her feel like a failure as a woman.

Gender Characteristics: Gender characteristics have developed over the centuries. Because they are so deeply ingrained in our culture, men and women may not even recognize them. However, being aware of these different characteristics makes it possible to avoid problems associated with them.

Women tend to personalize and blame themselves when there is a relationship problem: it must be their fault (see Blame- Self-Blame, Blame- Personalize). Ironically, they do this even if they also blame the man.

Stereotypically, they were culturally trained as children to avoid competition, to not stand out by winning. To win over a man might threaten what they have been taught is his fragile ego (see Fragile Ego). They were also culturally trained not to acknowledge or even recognize their own feelings of anger, because their job in relationships is to seek out and prevent problems (see Anger- Feelings, Competition, Cultural Roles).

The gender characteristics for men are less complex than for women. (Some research actually speculates this is related to the sexual organs: women's are internal and sexual pleasure requires internal probing; men's organs are external and more easily accessible.)

Men were trained to take care of those assumed to be less powerful, that is women and children. As in the animal kingdom, the male is more powerful and shows off his prowess – for animals, their beauty, for humans, their knowledge. If they fail, they experience shame. Men sense they must harness their anger because it can be dangerous; so they deny feeling it. If it can't be denied, they verbally (or physically) strike out at the woman or flee (see Anger- Actions, Anger- Feelings, Cultural Roles, Shame, Winner/Loser).

I Love You

Men and women need to hear the words, I love you, but they need to hear it in their own way. When you tell your partner about your love, you are giving a gift,

and gifts need to be given in the language of the Receiver (see Gift Giving).

When a man tells a woman he loves her, it needs to be in Female-ese. This means he tells her with words and compliments; he should use physical touch, not intercourse. He could do small personal things for her, like bring flowers, or leave notes or small surprises. He could buy her gifts. In fact, women have a wide range of how a man can show his love. Giving advice, a Male-ese way to show love, is not a substitute for the way she needs to hear it (see Advice).

A man is less fussy about how a woman can show she loves him. Words are fine, but making love with him may be the best way. He may also appreciate her buying him a tool he has always wanted, or doing a task like sewing on a button (see Cultural Roles).

I'm Fine

When a man or woman is asked how they are, the response may be, "I'm fine." But too often they are not really fine.

For women, "I'm fine" may mean "I'm really angry and hurt, but I won't talk to you about it. Besides, you ought to know what's wrong with me. It's your fault." (see Communication Style- Direct/Indirect).

For men, "I'm fine" may mean "I am feeling something intensely emotional (sad, lonely), and I don't want to recognize or admit how it makes me feel. I'm supposed to be manly and these intense emotions are unmanly" (see Emotional Pain). Or, it could mean "I'm feeling anger, but if I acknowledge it, I may lose control" (see Anger- Feelings).

While sometimes these two words mean just what they say, more often than not they require a Male-ese or Female-ese interpretation.

Intimacy

Intimacy has different meanings for men than for women. Not being aware of these differences can cause hurt feelings.

In Male-ese, intimacy means sex, the act of inter-course. While men have other intimacy desires, like wanting to be loved, valued, appreciated, and needed, the act of sex has become a catch-all term for these desires. Because of the male societal mandate, they often do not have the language to express their emotional needs (see Emotional Pain, Winner/Loser).

Intimacy, in Female-ese, means an emotional closeness that increases the desire for lovemaking (see Sex- Female Aphrodisiac, Sex- Pre-Foreplay, and Communication Style- Sharing Feelings). This differ-ence alone causes enormous miscommunication and/or anger. If women are not feeling emotionally close to a man, they may not be interested in sex. While both men and women want this closeness, women need to feel it before they desire sex; men often need the sex in order to feel the closeness. Both want emotional intimacy, but it's like the men wait at the train station while women are at the airport.

Another aspect of intimacy for women that is a mystery to many men has to do with the details of every-day life. Many women feel closer and more affectionate towards the man when they know the details of his daily life. This contributes to their love and connection. The details can be mundane, such as his routine for brushing his teeth, starting to drive before hooking his seat belt, or how and why he acts the way he does in certain situations. The more a woman knows about the man, the closer she feels to him, and this is an indication of their intimacy. In turn, the woman wants the man to understand everything about her, thinking it will make him feel as close as it makes her feel.

However, it doesn't always work this way. For a man, a woman knowing him that well does not necessarily produce closeness. Often it feels claustrophobic. Too much knowledge may leave the man feeling vulnerable, because she can see his failures or weaknesses. Furthermore, experiencing the depth of that closeness might flood him, leaving him feeling vulnerable, i.e., unmanly (see Shame, Winner/Loser).

I-Statements

An I-Statement means a person speaks from the position of his or her feelings. For example, "I was hurt when you didn't come home for dinner." This is only a statement of the speaker's feelings.

The opposite is a You-Statement, in which the speaker pronounces a judgment or criticism about what the other person has done or said, such as, "You didn't come home for dinner." This can be experienced as accusatory and an attack, which usually results in a counterattack.

The value of an I-Statement is that the other person cannot argue with it. It's the speaker's feeling, not a statement of fact. I-Statements are an important tool for ensuring good arguments (see Arguments- Good Argument, Epilogue- Good Arguments).

A variation of the I-Statement occurs when a person speaks not about feelings but from his or her own perception. The speaker is not saying the other person is wrong, only that the speaker has a different perception of a situation. Instead of, "You were rude to the waiter," it would be, "From my perspective, you were rude to the waiter." Other phrases that avoid an attack include "My version is," "As I see the situation," "My point of view is," and "From inside my shoes" (see Switching Shoes).

I-Statements help avoid an argument. And if both sides use I-Statements, the argument is cut short. The issue then isn't who is right or wrong, but how each person experiences the situation (see Control- I'm Right).

Caution: Avoid the Cheating I-Statement. This comes in the disguise of, "I feel you are wrong," or "I feel you should apologize to me." As you can see, it's really a You-Statement with the words "I feel" tacked in front. A true I-Statement, for instance, would be, "I'm hurt that you said/did that to me," instead of a demanding an apology.

Last Word

"You always have to have the last word!" This is an inflammatory phrase because of the absolute "always" and the accusatory "you" (see I-Statements, Never/ Always/Should).

The person, man or woman, using this phrase may be expressing desperation about not feeling heard or taken seriously. When people don't feel their partner hears their point of view, in their own gender language style, they may feel powerless, overridden, or discounted. After a while, these feelings can erode a sense of love and commitment.

To avoid this phrase, both partners need to talk about better ways for each to feel heard, without feeling as though they are being discounted, put down, or made the brunt of sarcasm (see Arguments- Good Argument).

There are playful ways to deal with an exchange in which both people want the last word. For instance, at the count of three, the two people simultaneously end the conversation. Another possibility is that the couple can alternate who gets the last word (see the example in Control- I'm Right).

Love/Hate

What's the opposite of love? Chances are men and women alike will answer, hate. But they would be wrong. The opposite of love is indifference. The opposite of hate (or intense anger) is also indifference. Love and hate are actually two sides of the same coin, the coin being "intense emotions." People don't hate their dry cleaner for ruining their suit. They may be angry and probably won't go back there again, but the feelings are not intense enough to qualify as hate. In personal relationships, people have to care enough to hate.

When people are afraid to feel the full extent of their anger, they actually prevent themselves from feeling the full extent of their love. When you sit on your anger at your partner, or deny you even feel the anger, you are snuffing out part of the intensity of your feelings. In fact, you are dulling your love.

Mentor

Men love mentoring women, helping them move ahead professionally. Giving advice as a mentor is not the same as giving unsolicited advice (see Advice). Through mentoring, a man can show his expertise in how a woman can, for example, ask for a raise, start her own business, go back to school, or apply for a job she modestly thinks is beyond her capability.

A man is successful as a mentor if the woman takes his advice, uses his energy, models his actions, and moves ahead. In fact, if a man is successful, he works himself out of his job as mentor. The woman grows through his efforts and no longer needs him as mentor. She needs him now as a colleague or just a supportive lover or husband.

However, a man may feel bad about the loss of his hierarchal role. He may be more comfortable being in a one-up position as the mentor rather than seeing the woman as an equal. He may subtly or openly discourage her progress. He may find fault with what she is doing or tell her how to do it better. This shift can strain or destroy a relationship.

Too often, if a woman sees (or imagines she sees) the man's hurt or negative reaction to no longer being needed, she may pull back from her own progress (see Fragile Ego). She might not take the promotion, might give up on returning to college, or drop her idea of starting her own business. She may worry that if she grows professionally, and he is left behind, he may feel bad or resentful. When that happens, she is reacting to her internalized message about protecting a man's fragile ego.

While she may be correct in assessing the man is feeling unneeded or inadequate as she moves ahead professionally, she will not know for sure if she doesn't talk to him about it. And if she is correct, by talking about it, they can discuss other ways she can show she needs him that are not at her own expense. Alternatively, her success could energize him to focus more on his own growth.

If the discussion is not successful, she needs to make a decision: keep growing and upset him, stop growing to keep the peace, or leave him.

Miscommunication

Miscommunication between a man and a woman can erupt from each stubbornly believing they are right and refusing to hear the other's point of view (see I'm Right). This can also happen when the partners mishear what the other is saying. This type of miscommunication comes from either not making sure you each understand the other's perspective, or not listening carefully enough without pre-judgments (see Arguments- Good Argument, I-Statements).

Listening to the other does not mean you have to accept or agree with the other's perspective. It simply means you hear what the other person is saying correctly, and you understand the other person's intended meaning (see Appendices 2 and 3).

The Miscommunication Cycle: When a woman is upset with a man, she tells him why and expects him to explain himself, apologize, or at least give his opinion. She waits for his response for what seems to her to be a long enough time for him to say something if he wanted to. When the man remains silent, she thinks she must not have explained herself well enough, so she continues, sometimes going on to other complaints (see Conversation- Silence, Time/Timing).

The man, however, doesn't experience her pause as stopping. To him it seems just a moment, just enough time to catch her breath. So he sits silently, waiting for her to finish. For him, the indicator of her being finished would be a question he can answer. Without that question, he doesn't know what she is looking for. So he waits. For men, conversations are about reporting information (see Conversation- Purpose). Without the question, he thinks she is simply reporting information and not looking for anything from him (see We Have to Talk. About What?).

This cycle — the woman talking, waiting for the man to respond, when he doesn't, she continues — can go on for a long time, with her talking for longer periods and him sitting and waiting for longer periods of time. Over the years of being together, couples often have reinforced each other's patterns. He no longer expects her to stop talking and ask him a question; she no longer expects him to respond to her.

An easy technique to get past the Male-ese and Female-ese differences is the "Period." When the women is finished speaking, when she expects the man to respond, she says, "Period." Or conversely, when the man suspects she may be finished, he can say, "Is that a period?" Another way to use this exercise is that, when the woman is going on and on and the man thinks she is repeating herself, the man can say, "I need a period."

Question behind the Question: This is a technique that both men and women can use to avoid miscommunication. The following joke illustrates this point. A young child asks his parents where he comes from. After parents give a lengthy discussion of eggs and sperm and briefly

pause, the child asks, "Was I born in Minneapolis or St. Paul?" Whenever there's any doubt about the meaning of a question, asking, "What's the question behind the question," can be quite helpful.

For example, if the man asks, "Are you going to the library?" the woman might feel defensive, thinking he is implying she should not go so often. Or she might feel attacked, thinking that he is blaming her for going instead of doing something with him. Rather than trying to guess the meaning of his question, if she asks, "What's the question behind the question?" she might learn he has a book on reserve and would like her to pick it up for him. In other words, until she asks for more information, she may react negatively to an innocent question.

Name Calling

In the midst of an argument, many partners resort to what may be the most subtle form of name calling: "You're just like your mother/father!" This may be even more inflammatory than swear words. Even if it's true, stating the comparison does not enhance the argument.

When a man or woman feels helpless or powerless in making a point, this form of name calling serves only to attack; it is not used to clarify a situation. Telling you partner, "You're just like your mother/father," is like wielding a big gun on your side.

Never/Always/Should (see Arguments- Good Argument)

Never/Always/Should, along with Must, Need to, and Have To are dangerous words in an argument. They are either absolutes, which are usually inaccurate, or commands and challenges, which no one likes. Using any of these words is like throwing a red flag in front of a bull. It's a challenge to fight in order to gain control.

The use of these words drags in past arguments and moves away from the current topic. A good argument stays focused only on the present issue.

Pleasing the Other

When men and women want to show their love and consideration for each other, they tend to do it in their own gendered style (see Gift Giving).

When men give advice or do a task, like taking care of their partner's car, their intent is to please her (see

Advice). She, however, may be annoyed. While she may appreciate a man checking her oil level, that hardly counts as doing something to please her, because it's not personal.

A woman also wants to please a man by doing things for him. She may attend to what she imagines he might be feeling. If she is wrong, he is likely to be offended or feel controlled. If she is right, he might feel emotionally exposed, and hence resentful.

When women do something concrete to please a man, like turn on a light while he is reading, he may appreciate her effort, or he might be annoyed, thinking, "If I need the light, I can turn it on myself." Her doing something he could do for himself may come too close to making him feel like a child (see Shame, Winner/Loser).

If the pleasing is not done in the gendered style, rather than appreciating each other's efforts, the Receiver is annoyed, and the Giver feels hurt and unappreciated.

The Double Bind in Pleasing a Woman: Female-ese sets a trap for men. A woman asks a man to do something for her or with her. He says fine. She then complains, "You're only doing this to please me." In fact, he may only be doing it to please her. But, what's so wrong with that? Men and women often do things for the other, just to please them.

But if the man admits he's doing it just to please her, she may be angry or feel guilty that he is not doing what he wants. She doesn't accept what he wants is to please her.

Women need to appreciate and accept that when men try to please them, this is another form of giving;

they need to graciously say, "Thank you" (see Thank you).

Pronouns

Research shows when women talk about a situation involving themselves and their partner, they use the plural pronouns, "we," and "us."

When men talk about the exact same situation, they might use the singular pronouns, "I" and "me." They are not intentionally excluding women; in Maleese, they tend to speak solely from their own position. Since women tend to personalize anything having to do with relationships, when a woman hears her partner say "I," she may feel excluded or ignored, a sign he doesn't love her (see Blame-Personalize, Qtip).

QTIP (see Blame- Personalize)

Quit Taking It Personally! QTIP is an important tool to use in relationships, especially for women, who tend to personalize far too many of men's comments and behaviors. Women would do well to write down these 4 letters and paste them on their mirrors, their desks, or even their car dashboard.

Many arguments occur because women unnecessarily personalize the man's comments, instead of telling themselves to QTIP.

Relationship Expectations

When people know how they want their partner to act or respond in a given situation, they may be setting themselves up for disappointment or anger. Too often, their expectations are not in line with their partner's, even when there are simple things like: "If only she would hug me when I come home from the office," or "I have told him numerous times I would like him to brush my hair while we're watching TV."

It is important for partners to be direct and clear about what they want (see Communication Style-Direct/Indirect). If, after several discussions about one's expectations, the partner still is not doing what was asked, the person has two choices: to continue to ask and be disappointed or angry or to change the expectations.

People need to accept the fact that although their partner is good and loving in many ways, they may not behave according to particular expectations. When one gives up expecting what is not going to happen, there is no need for blame or sizzling resentment. When expectations are removed, both partners can accept what they have in each other, ignore what they don't like, and *stop wanting what they know they will never get.* (See my article, "Three Steps to Stop Kvetching About Men," at http://www.DrKGL.com/kvetch.)

Shoebox and Mantel: The difference between men and women in their attitude towards relationships can be compared to how they each handle a precious treasure. When a man has a treasure (like his relationship), he gently wraps it up in something soft and lays it in a shoebox that he tucks under his bed. He knows where it is; he knows it's safe, so he doesn't have to think about it anymore. If he ever wants to, he can get it out, but he doesn't need to because he knows it's safely tucked away. He doesn't need to display it.

On the other hand, when a woman has a treasure (like her relationship), she displays it on the mantel. She looks at it every time she goes by, she dusts it, rearranges it, and shows it off when people come over. She needs the something special to be visible so it can be appreciated.

Men don't believe they have to show the woman they appreciate her, while women want overt and frequent indications of being appreciated.

These gender-based differences are often a key ingredient to relationship conflict and hurt. Grasping their significance and consciously making changes can help avoid unnecessary pain.

The problem is not that men and women have different expectations; the problem is people continue pressing for their expectations long after it is clear they are not going to be met.

Relaxation after Work

In dual career families, men and women often have different ways of relaxing after a stressful day, ways that may not be compatible. Upon immediate entry into the home, even if they have children, men need time to unwind. This may include changing clothes, reading the paper, or running on the treadmill.

When women come home, they don't feel they have the luxury of unwinding. The children need attention, dinner has to be made, phone calls need to be returned. Even if the man makes the dinner, women often carry the responsibility of getting the laundry done, making the children's lunches for the next day, finding carpools for the children's activities. And of course, there's always the children's homework.

Men may participate in the same chores, but they may set a different sequence. They may relax first and then get to the chores. Or they participate in getting dinner made and homework done, but afterwards, they relax. That may be when they want the woman to join them, as they unwind in front of the television.

However, for women, watching television may seem like something to be done only after the chores are complete. So, some women resent their husband for wasting time and relaxing. But of course, chores are never completed.

A man often experiences his wife's refusal to sit and relax with him as a personal rejection; she doesn't want to spend time with him.

When a woman does take time to relax, she is more likely to want to take a walk with the man (where they can talk) or just sit and talk. While talking can be calming for women, for many men, it is stressful (see Communication Style, Conversation- Silence).

The lack of awareness of these gender differences too often leaves both men and women wanting to relax together, yet feeling the other is rejecting their offer.

Sex

There are many components of sex and each has specific gender differences. A satisfactory sexual encounter requires attention to both the Male-ese and Female-ese experience in each of the components.

Pre-Foreplay: Most men know a woman requires foreplay before she is ready for intercourse. However, many women need something else before foreplay; they need what can be called "pre-foreplay."

Pre-Foreplay is the time before the beginning of making love, the transition time a man and women spend together, which entails letting go of everyday concerns and reconnecting with each other. Many women need this transition to get in the mood to even think about making love. Pre-Foreplay, then, helps them clear their mind of work, children's soccer schedules, the caretaking of their aging parents, bills, or even remembering Thurs‧ day is trash day. Men may not realize this since they have less need for transitioning.

Pre-Foreplay may include taking a walk together (but not talking about anything personal or serious), taking a bath together (without anything sexual), or playing a game of bingo or cards. What a couple does together is far less important than being together and letting go of the everyday "stuff." Only then are women ready for foreplay.

Female Aphrodisiac: This is a form of Pre-Fore-play. Sometimes women need or want additional non-sexual stimuli before Foreplay. They need what is called an aphrodisiac.

One primary female aphrodisiac is a four letter word that ends in K, but does not start with an F; it's... Talk. All the romantic dinners and diamonds in the world won't arouse a woman's sexual desire for a man as quickly, or as consistently, as an emotional conversation (see Conversation- Purpose, Communication Style- Sharing Feelings). A woman's desire increases when a man talks about his feelings and listens to hers. To her, talking means he is sensitive, in touch with his feelings, and cares enough about her to want to share. It allows her to feel connected to him. Talking is a turn-on that leads to a woman feeling sexually excited and aroused.

Kiss as Foreplay: Mouth-to-mouth kissing is the forgotten ingredient in lovemaking, especially for couples who have been together for a long time. For men, kissing is a part of the whole process of lovemaking, but it often does not carrying any significant value.

For women, though, kissing is a crucial element in foreplay. A slow tender kiss of deep passion may be an intimate and highly arousing experience; sometimes it is the quickest route to sexual arousal. Many women claim to have orgasms just from mouth-to-mouth kissing, perhaps because the kiss leads women to feel a deep connection to the man. (See my article, "6 Types of Kisses – From Passion to Empty Air," at http://www.DrKGL.com/kiss.)

For menopausal women with lowered libido, the emotional connection of pre-foreplay and kissing as foreplay are especially important, as they facilitate sexual arousal.

Emotional Connection: When men let their guard down and share their emotions, they risk feeling vulnerable or weak. This is more tolerable after they have had the physical connection of sex. After intercourse, they are more willing to talk about personal feelings and to express deep emotions.

For women, it's just the opposite. In order to want sex, they need to feel emotionally close to the man first. Before getting to the bedroom, a woman needs to see that he loves her and is willing to share his feelings. He needs to make her feel cherished and loved. Then a woman is ready and willing to make love (see Intimacy). This is another example of men waiting at the train station while the women are at the airport.

Intercourse: In the act of intercourse, men think they should know how to please the woman. This belief is fed by the societal pressure on them: "real men" know what women want. Those who have been sexually active in prior relationships are even more bound by this belief.

Men are caught between two contradictory Male-ese messages: they are supposed to know about women's sexual needs, and they are not supposed to ask questions. Whatever they do, they risk feeling shamed for being wrong (see Conversation- Questions, Shame, Winner/Loser).

Yet, when men do ask women what they like or if something pleases them, they may be foiled. From childhood on, women have been trained not to hurt a man's ego, so they let the man believe he is satisfying them (see Fragile Ego). Their Female-ese training says the man should take the lead. For women to be more assertive goes against their childhood messages saying, "If you are interested in sex, you must be a slut." So, women tend not to take steps to ensure their own satisfaction.

One of those steps might include exploring their own body. But many women were brought up believing it was bad to masturbate and explore their body. Therefore, they cannot help a man satisfy them because they themselves do not know what pleases them.

Even when women do know what will please them, they often speak so vaguely, the man does not get the message (see Communication Style- Direct/Indirect).

Furthermore, if women are direct in telling a man what they need, but he does not listen, they will rarely speak up a second time. To do so, many women feel, would hurt the man's ego (see Fragile Ego).

When a woman does not speak up directly to get her sexual satisfaction, the man erroneously thinks he is pleasing her. Unfortunately, the woman then may blame him for being insensitive to her.

Clearly, communication is more crucial to sexual satisfaction for both men and women than the actual act of intercourse. In fact, intercourse is only satisfying when all these other elements of sex have first been met.

Shame

Everyone feels shame at times, but for men it has unique dynamics. Shame is directly related to the messages passed down through the generations: men must be winners, should not be weak, should not be vulnerable, and should stay in control of their emotions (see Communication Style- Sharing Feelings, Emotional Pain, Winner/Loser). By default, not adhering to these rules makes a man a loser, and thus he feels shame.

Men may feel shame when they experience a yearning for a connection with a woman; it makes them feel weak and needy, thus vulnerable.

They feel shame when they have lost control of their anger and yell or throw things (see Anger- Actions). They may compensate for this shame by later being very loving.

To avoid feeling shame, men may avoid certain situations so they do not get flooded with their anger. This explains why men walk out of a room in the middle of an argument. Or why they can suddenly go silent in the middle of a conversation, as if they have shut down internally, which is exactly what they have done. Silence calms the internal emotional turmoil, and helps them avoid becoming out of control (see Anger- Actions, Stress and Physiology, Silence).

Switching Shoes

Switching Shoes is a tool to help couples resolve conflict. It is a way of metaphorically seeing what the situation looks like from another person's perspective.

Arguments are not bad; they are only bad when not handled well. Unfortunately, arguments often occur when both sides think what they are saying is correct and what the other person is saying is wrong. In this case, both sides try harder and harder to convince the other of their rightness (see Control- I'm Right). And of course, that never happens.

The way to switch shoes is for both people to present the other's side of the argument – as if it were their own. Taking the opposite position helps them each understand the other's point of view. This does not mean they like the other's point of view, but at least they can see how the other came to it. Standing in each other's shoes removes the need for a winner and a loser. Both can be winners (see Arguments- Good Argument, I-Statements).

Tears

Tears and crying are not always synonymous for men and women. For women, tears may be an expression of sadness, grief, loneliness, or hurt.

However, tears may also be an expression of anger. Women have been socialized that anger is unfeminine, aggressive. As a result, they may repress their feelings of anger and only be aware of sadness (see Anger-Feelings).

In an argument with a man, a woman may shed angry tears. A man, assuming they are tears of sadness, may be moved to comfort her. At other times, he may see the tears as a manipulation in order to win her point.

For themselves, men usually see tears as a sign of weakness — whether they are tears of physical pain or emotional distress (see Emotional Pain). Therefore, tears are to be avoided if at all possible, and the emotion should be diverted to a more acceptable emotion, like anger, frustration, or even silence. Men may also burn off the emotion through physical activity. Finally, they might numb the emotion and the associated tears through a mindless activity like television, computer games, or the use of alcohol.

Men need to understand what the tears represent when women cry. And women need to understand what men's distancing or anger represents. To have a meaningful appreciation for each other's feelings, men and women first need to learn the meanings behind their own behaviors. Too often, neither men nor women are clear about what they are truly feeling.

Thank You

Women often have a hard time accepting a compliment (from men and from women) and just saying, "Thank you." A man says something nice about a woman's dress or a meal she has prepared, and a woman has a self-put-down ready. "Oh, this old thing," she may say, or "It was really nothing; I just threw some things together (see Compliments)." This drives men crazy.

Conversely, women want to be appreciated and thanked for doing something special for a man. They want their efforts to be noted. Because men don't need the same degree of verbalized appreciation, they are less likely to give it to a woman. This conflict in style can cause serious discord (see Gift Giving, Pleasing the Other, Relationship Expectations- Shoebox and Mantel).

Time/Timing

A potential relationship problem that is not related to gender is the reality that people run on different internal clocks. "You're always late." "You're always racing around; it drives me crazy." "You are so pokey; it takes you hours to do the simplest thing."

Ironically, people with a slower internal clock are often partnered with those with a faster one. The problem arises when each expects the other to change (see Relationship Expectations). In fact, internal clocks may be slightly adjusted or temporarily shifted, but they cannot be reset.

Therefore, couples need to acknowledge their different internal timing without trying to change each other. For instance, a faster person annoyed by a partner consistently running late can drive to events separately rather than continually complain.

When the faster partner races around the house, the slower partner can take deep breaths and keep busy with something else rather than yell, "Slow down, you're making me nervous."

Timing in Arguments: People also have different internal clocks for dealing with arguments. The ones who process feelings faster will want to discuss the issue right away. They often are partnered with someone who, as a slower processer, needs a few hours or a day to gather thoughts before being ready for a discussion. Without an immediate discussion, the faster one may feel unheard or discounted. Yet, the slower processor, if forced into a discussion, may go silent.

Couples benefit by recognizing their timing differences. The slower processors might say, "I hear you, and I need time to think about my response. Let's talk tomorrow right after dinner." The faster processors usually are fine with the delay as long as they know they will be getting back to the issue at a specified time (see Epilogue- Good Argument).

We Have to Talk. About What?

Joke: What are the four words that put terror in a man's heart?

Answer: We have to talk.

Many women freely tell a man why they are upset with him. They may describe a situation or several situations. They explain what he did or didn't do. When finished, they often ask some open-ended question like, "So, what do you think?" or "What do you have to say?" A man's response to such a question is usually "About what?"

This drives women crazy! How can he not know, they think. They assume he answered that way just to anger them (see Blame- Personalize). But the man's confusion is real. Women can cover a lot of topics in their complaints, and if they don't end with a specific question, the man doesn't know to what he is responding (see Conversation- Questions).

What works better is for women to lay out one or two specific complaints, without accusation, and to end with a specific question — even if it's only, "Do you have an idea how we can avoid this next time?" (See

Argument- Good Arguments, Epilogue- Good Argument.)

Why Did You…?

In an argument, people usually ask why the other person did or said something because they want to prove the other wrong or validate their own position. Asking why can be inflammatory and opens the door for a counterattack against the other (see Arguments- Deflect the Conversation, Arguments- Tit for Tat). One or both people end up feeling blamed, and nothing changes the situation for the future. For women, avoiding this question is particularly hard since they like to process situations involving their feelings. However, asking "Why Did You…?" is often not helpful.

What is more helpful is to make sure whatever happened is avoided in the future. The discussion, then, can be future-focused, rather than looking back. A better question, for instance, would be, "What can we do differently next time so this won't happen?"

Winner/Loser (see Arguments- Deflect the Conversation, Arguments- Dirty Fighting, Arguments- Tit for Tat, Blame- Externalize/Internalize, Shame)

From early childhood, boys are indoctrinated into the male hierarchical social order of "One-Up" or "One-Down." This means there are only two positions: the winner and the loser. If a boy is not a winner, by default, he is a loser.

This societal mandate is reinforced in boys by the injunction, "Big boys don't cry." If a boy is the loser in games, physical fights, or even not being picked for the spelling team, the unspoken code states he shouldn't cry. It also states if he is the winner, he can't show empathy for the loser. Especially among young boys where there is the fear of contagion: if he shows empathy for the loser, he might be seen as a loser. While the playground and group sports have changed in recent decades, the mandate remains, albeit more subtly.

There are many ways the Winner/Loser mandate, absorbed from childhood, can be detrimental to men in their love relationships. For instance:

- "Be a winner, not a loser" gets translated as "get or keep the upper hand." Yet, men often feel they do not have the upper hand in emotionally charged conversations.
- Concern about being in the one-down position may lead men to avoid emotional conversations, or to shift into a tit for tat or counter-attack of blaming the woman. Or, they may just leave the room.
- When men feel verbally attacked or challenged by their partner, they are faced with two options. They can fight back, but risk getting emotionally out of control, which is only for losers. Or, they can walk away.
- Winners do not expose their vulnerability, which is what many women want in a love relationship.

- Winners avoid showing their need for nurturing. So, when a woman reaches out in a nurturing or caretaking way, men may recoil, fearing they are being treated like a child.
- Winners are never in a one-down position; this may explain why so many men have difficulty with apologizing, saying "I'm sorry.
- When men first meet a woman, they may talk too much about themselves. While a woman might see them as self-centered, they may only be reacting to the winner mandate by demonstrating their accomplishments or knowledge.

Obviously, not all men obey these social rules all the time, but it's important for both men and women to recognize when they bump into the Winner/Loser mandate.

EPILOGUE

Now that you are familiar with Male-ese and Female-ese, let's go back to the three couples from the Prologue and see what caused their conflicts and misunderstandings.

First, each of the exchanges is repeated from the Prologue. But, in parentheses are the dictionary terms causing problems. This is followed by The Male-ese and Female-ese Issues which explains the problems caused by each term. Finally, there is A Bilingual Conversation that shows how each couple could have handled the situation differently if they were tuned in to the gendered language differences.

Couple 1: After the Party

"Ok. What's up?" He sighs, "You've been quiet ever since we left home this evening. I thought it was a great party, but you've been pouty."

"I'm not pouty," she pouts. (**Indirect**)

"Come off it, of course you are. Something's been bothering you from the moment we got in the car."

"No," she corrects him. "From the moment I came down the stairs ready to go, and you didn't say a thing about how I looked." Her eyes tear up. (**No I-Statement**)

"Huh? Is that what this is about? Is that why you didn't speak to me the whole drive over and looked so hurt look all evening?" (**Question**) He's exasperated. "You looked lovely; you always do. I'm always proud of how you look."

"You didn't tell me." Against her best intentions, there is a slight whine.

"You didn't ask." (**Shoebox and Mantel**)

"You should tell me without my having to ask." (**Never/Always/ Should**) The whine is louder now. "Otherwise, I don't know if you are just saying it because I want to hear it." (**Compliment**)

The Male-ese and Female-ese Issues:

Indirect: The woman was not being direct in saying what she wanted from him. The man, therefore, totally missed what she was asking.

I-Statement: There was no "I" in her sentence, speaking from her perspective. There was just the complaint about what he didn't do.

Question: This is good – as far as it went. At least he was questioning why she didn't speak to him.

Shoebox and Mantel: She wanted him to show his love "Mantel" style; his love, though, was comfortably tucked away in his "Shoebox."

Never/Always/Should: Any sentence that begins with "You should..." is off to a bad start. It can only go downhill from there.

Compliment: This is a trap; he can't win whether he says something or not.

A Bilingual Conversation

Before they went to the party, this is how their conversation might have gone:

Woman: "How do I look in this outfit?" (**Direct**)

Man: "You look lovely; you always do. I'm always proud of how you look." (**Shoebox and Mantel**)

Woman: "I'm glad, but I'm talking about right now, not in general. Do you like the way this looks on me?" (**Direct**)

Man: "Yes."

Since he has told her this other times she has worn this dress, he figures there might be something else going on. "Is there something else you are trying to hear from me?" (**Question**)

Woman: "Well, I guess I'm a bit nervous about this party. Your old girlfriend will be there, so I want to make sure we are feeling good about each other before arriving there, so I won't be jealous." (**I-Statement**)

Couple 2: The Flowers

They sit in my office glaring at each other.

He finally growls, "I can never do enough for you; it's one complaint after another. I know women like flowers, so I bring you roses, but even that wasn't right. You never even put them in a vase. After a while, I just gave up." (**Questions, If It Ain't Broke**)

She says, "I didn't say anything the first two times you brought me flowers because I thought it was romantic, and I didn't want to hurt your feelings. (**Fragile Ego**) But the third time, I reminded you I'm allergic to them. You never listened to me (**Never/Always/**

Should) and kept giving them to me for Valentine's Day, or just as an "I love you" surprise. (**Gift Giving**) So, I'd just put them aside. The flowers just became another example of how you never listen." (**Never/Always/ Should**)

The Male-ese and Female-ese Issues

Questions: He missed an obvious clue. After the first few times, even after the first time, he noticed she didn't put the flowers in a vase. At that time, he could have asked if there was a problem.

If It Ain't Broke: Perhaps he didn't ask why she didn't put the flowers in water because he didn't want to risk it becoming a bigger problem.

Fragile Ego: She didn't speak up the first time he brought her flowers for fear of hurting his feelings. So by the third time, she was really angry. If she had spoken up at first, she wouldn't be harboring the growing anger.

Never/Always/Should: She globalized him not listening to her; she didn't stick to this specific situation.

Gift Giving: He was giving her a gift, the flowers, in the way he wanted to do it. He did not think about whether it was in her style.

A Bilingual Conversation

This is how their conversation might have gone, initiated by either the man or the woman:

Man: "I am curious why you are not putting the flowers in water. Is there a problem?" (**I-Statement, Questions**)

OR

Woman: "I appreciate you giving me flowers because I know that means you care. But, I have told you I am allergic to them. Perhaps I wasn't clear or you forgot last time. By all means, do continue doing nice things showing me you care, but please don't do it with flowers." (**Direct, I-Statements**)

Couple 3: The Movies

One overcast Sunday afternoon, she asks, "What movie should we rent tonight?"

He, being glued to the TV, suggests, "How about King Kong?" (**Listening**)

Silence. Then she says, "I've never seen any of the Humphrey Bogart movies." (**Indirect**)

Not taking his eyes from the football game, he absentmindedly says, "That's fine; whatever you want." (**Listening, Purpose of Conversation, Question, Verbal Tennis**) She snaps, "You never listen to me." (**I-Statements, Never/Always/Should**)

His head jerks up, now looking directly at her. First surprise, then anger flash in his eyes. (**Shame, Winner/Loser**) "Oh, for chrissake! What's the big deal? You didn't listen to me about buying that new blender. (**Tit for Tat**) I couldn't care less which movie we see. In fact, I don't care if we see one or not!" (**Anger**) As he storms out of the room, he shouts, "You're never satisfied; you always have to pick on me." (**Never/Always/Should, Shame, Stress and Physiology, Winner/Lose**)

The Male-ese and Female-ese Issues

Listening: When he does not look at her as she is talking, she feels he isn't connecting with her, that he really isn't paying attention.

Indirect: She made a statement about the Bogart movie that only implied her wish to see it. She was not attuned to the Male-ese need to have a specific question.

Purpose of Conversation: When she asked his preference, she expected he would ask her preference in return. The purpose of conversation for her is the exchange of ideas, while for him it is to report information, answer a question.

Question: He was not attuned to the Female-ese about questions; she wanted her question returned – as in **Verbal Tennis**.

I-Statement: She does not say how she feels about him not listening to her, as in "I feel ignored," or "I hate it when I speak to you and you don't respond." By saying, "You never listen," she makes a "You-Statement."

Never/Always/Should: The absolute "Never" is inflammatory and does not stick to the conversation at hand.

Shame: When he exploded and fled the room, he probably felt shame at having let his emotions get so out of control.

Winner/Loser: Her comment felt like an accusation, that he had done something wrong; he felt like a loser.

Tit for Tat: When he felt attacked, he counterattacked by bringing up a totally unrelated issue to the topic at hand.

Anger: He did not separate his feeling of anger from whatever action he decided to take because of his feeling anger. He jumped right into action.

Stress and Physiology: Physiologically, his stress level increased and his reaction was to flee rather than further explode.

A Bilingual Conversation

This is how their conversation might have gone if they were both attuned to Male-ese and Female-ese:

Woman: "What movie would you like to rent tonight?"

Man taking his eyes off the TV: "How about a King Kong film? What would you like to see?" (**Listening, Verbal Tennis. Question**)

Woman: "King Kong is fine."

OR

Woman: "King Kong is fine, but I've never seen any of the Humphrey Bogart movies. I'd prefer one of them instead." (**Direct**)

Man, taking his eyes off TV again: "Bogie is fine with me." (**Listening**)

OR

Woman: "What movie would you like to rent tonight?"

Man, taking his eyes off the TV: "This isn't the best time for me to think about this. How about we talk about this in 15 minutes, during the break?" (**Listening, Timing**)

THE GOOD ARGUMENT

Now that you have learned to think bilingually, it's time for you to put it all together. Here are three examples of how couples can have a good argument.

In, **We have To Talk,** there are two options for how the couple could respond, including how the woman got the conversation back on track when the man was defensive and inflammatory.

The **Remove the Nagging** example shows how the man avoided getting sucked into feeling nagged and got the conversation back on track.

The third example, **Men: An Alternative to Giving Advice**, is a practice exercise where you can apply what you have learned and come up with your own ideas for understanding and using Male-ese and Female-ese.

We Have To Talk

Woman: "This is how I feel. I'm telling you this from my perspective. For weeks, you come home late. Lots of nights, you miss dinner and putting the kids to bed. On weekends, you are too tired to spend time with the kids, or you have more work to do. I feel you neglect the kids. I also feel you neglect me. Is there a problem between us? Or, is there something I'm missing in understanding why you can't be with me and us more?"

This is all from her perspective, and she uses only I-Statements. She ends with two questions focused on the problem. She does not ask why he's doing this. She does not accuse him of anything.

Man: "It's true. I do miss a lot of dinners and frankly, I miss not spending time with the kids in the evenings and not putting them to bed. And, you're right about the weekends. I am so tired I can hardly get out of bed. Or, what's even worse, I'm under pressure to get more work done before Monday.

"Let me reassure you: I love you and the kids very much. I'm not having an affair, and I'm not hiding out at work to avoid you. I don't know how to manage the time so I can get my work done and still have time to be with my family. I worry if I take time off, I'll lose this big contract (my boss will fire me/I'll get a bad evaluation, etc.)."

He remembers not to be defensive. He acknowledges her perception that he works too much and isn't home with her and the kids. He addresses what could be her underlying fear: he does love her and is not avoiding her. He explains why he works so much, without asking her to understand or forgive.

OR

Man: "You're always picking on me. What, you think I love working so late? I do it because you need new clothes and the kids have to have skating lessons and football outfits. You want vacations. Who's going to pay for all this if I don't work so hard? You want to go back to work and I'll stay home?"

His response is inflammatory. He is being defensive, he counterattacks, and he uses "You-Statements."

Woman: (defusing his defensiveness) "Wait. Let's start over again. I'm not accusing you of anything. In fact, I do appreciate how hard you work; I appreciate your making it possible for me to stay home and for us to have vacations and the kids get everything they need. You are a great provider. So, let me try again because I'm not attacking you. I'm only trying to let you know I want us to spend more time together. I miss you. I guess I need to know if you miss me, or if you are ok with us not spending any personal time together."

She does not absorb his counterattack; she sticks with I-Statements and addresses the concerns he raised in his counterattack – not feeling valued. Then, she goes back to her initial concern.

Man: "I'm sorry. I guess I was defensive. I work so hard and most of the time I don't feel appreciated – by my boss/clients or by you and the kids."

He apologizes, then stops himself from what could be a downward spiraling of his counterattacks, and explains the reason for his behavior – not feeling appreciated.

Woman: "You have reason to feel unappreciated by me, because I don't tell you enough how much I value what you do for us. I guess the question is, is there a way we can spend some quality time together – you and I —

as well as all of us as a family? Is there something I can do to help make it happen?"

She avoids a Tit for Tat that he doesn't value everything she does for him and the kids. She can tackle that another day, not in the middle of this particular argument. Instead, she sticks to the current issue, acknowledging his feeling unappreciated. She ends with a question that takes them forward into problem solving.

Man: (Still feeling pressured) "I apologize for getting testy. I feel helpless, and I feel attacked, and I can't spread myself thinner to do everything for everyone."

He shares the feelings underlying his defensivenes. He did not respond to her question of whether she could be of help.

Woman: "Is there some way we can talk about this, without your feeling like I'm attacking you or you getting defensive? Can we talk about what might work better for me but also for you, so you won't feel so torn?"

She lets him know that he doesn't have to do it all alone, reminding him they are on the same team.

Man: "I don't know how, but sure, if you think talking might help. But, frankly, I don't see any way out. If I did, I'd do it. Now, of course, is not a good time. But how about tomorrow – nope, I have to work late again. Ok. I promise I'll be free on Sunday morning. How's 10:30?"

Although skeptical, he is willing to hear her ideas, not being so competitive that he has to be the one to solve the problem. He proposes they talk later, at a specified time.

Woman: "That works fine for me. I'll make sure the kids won't interrupt us. I'll also do some thinking before then. If we put our heads together, maybe we can creatively find a way for you to do the work you need to do and for me to get more time with the husband I love."

Women: Ways to Remove the Nagging

Woman: (forgetting to use her bi-lingual lessons) "How many times do I have to ask you to clean out your junk in the basement? How are we supposed to get the leak fixed if your stuff is all over the place?"
She immediately forces the man into a defensive position with "You-Statements" and attacks.

Man: "Whoa. Can we start this conversation again? I think you are asking me to go through the boxes that are mine in the basement. We both have to go through our boxes, so what is your time line for this?"
He gets them back on track without a Tit for Tat.

Woman: "I'm so sorry. I totally forgot and was being mean. I am just worried about getting the basement cleaned up before the men come next week. We have to have it all packed up and stored elsewhere before then."
She apologizes and explains why she is so anxious.

Practice Exercise
Men: An Alternative to Giving Advice

Eva tells this story:

"My boss called me into his office. I assumed it was about a promotion or at least a raise. I was flabbergasted when he fired me! Practically stumbling out of the office, I drove straight home and immediately called Doug. I wanted sympathy, but his first reaction was, 'File a grievance.' I started to explain I didn't want advice or a suggestion, but he said it wasn't a good time to talk; he said we'd talk when he got home after work."

Put on your Male-ese thinking cap:
1. What do you think Doug was feeling when he got the call?
2. What do you think was behind his suggestion to file a grievance?
3. What do you think he might have been thinking when he said it wasn't a good time to talk, and they'd talk when he got home?
4. What else could Doug have done – given he did not believe he could leave the office at that moment?

Eva is outraged.

"I know he loves me, but I was furious. I had just been fired, and this was the best he could do? So I called my best friend, Patty. She said she'd rearrange her afternoon appointments and meet me in two hours. Now, that's true love!"

Put on your Female-ese thinking cap:

1. Why did Doug's reaction make Eva so angry?
2. What message did Eva get from Doug's first reaction, which was "to file a grievance"?
3. What would she have rather had him say?
4. She called her friend to get what she needed; that was good. What should she say to him when they talk in the evening?

APPENDIX 1

How to Think Bilingually in Your Relationship

1. Learn your own language first (Male-ese, Female-ese).
2. Learn the language of your mate.
3. Have clean, honest discussions about how to improve communication.
4. Make changes in yourself: you *can't* change anyone else.
5. Quitchabitchin' — After you've done steps 1-4, stop complaining. Assess your relationship expectations. Then, find a way to live with the person – or leave. Do not just stay and continue complaining, hoping the person will change.
6. Women: Quit Taking It Personally. Keep questioning how much you take things personally. When you feel offended you may, in fact, simply be hearing through Female-ese. The man may have been talking Male-ese and intended no insult.
7. Practice Listening and Switching Shoes.
8. When stuck in a conversation, reread the Gender Relationship Dictionary.

APPENDIX 2

Women: Steps to Avoid Miscommunication

These steps are for women when they want to initiate a personal conversation with a man. They are written with specific attention to the Male-ese needs for communication.

1. Pick only one topic to discuss at a time. Be specific.
2. Make sure you have his attention before you broach the need for a discussion. Do it during a quiet time, not while you are in the midst of an argument; and not when he is reading, on the computer, or otherwise occupied. Wait until you have eye contact with him and his undivided attention before you start talking. The purpose of this communication is to tell him you want to have a discussion on a particular topic.
3. Set an agreed upon time to meet. Be specific as to day, hour, and location.
4. Set the length of time to talk – between 30-60 minutes. If you need more, schedule for another time.
5. Come prepared, preferably having the issue you are concerned about in writing. Make it no more then 3-4 sentences.
6. Practice how you want to say it. (This will keep you focused and attuned to Male-ese.)

7. Use I-Statements.
8. Avoid absolutes like "always," "never," and commands like "should," and "have/must/need to."
9. Repeat back what he says to make sure you understand his point before you present your own point or take issue with his. Do this for each of his statements. Have him do it for your statements.
10. Stay focused on a solution that will help you avoid a similar problem next time. Do not bring up any past situations.
11. Do not be defensive. If at all possible, do not ask about or discuss why something happened. (When the man has to explain why he said or did something, it puts him on the defensive, and it keeps the focus backward, which opens you both up to more dissention.
12. Avoid getting emotional. Keep the tone matter-of-fact. Tears as well as yelling and sarcasm interfere with problem-solving.
13. Make sure you end with concrete ways to handle the situation this time and in the future. Write down your agreement so there will be no misunderstanding at some later point.
14. Make sure you end with a hug and/or a handshake.
15. Remember, you love each other. You are not enemy combatants; you are on the same team.

If you do this well, you will end up feeling more love and affection, knowing he has worked with you, not against you, to deal with an issue of great concern for you.

Do not be surprised if he wants to make love now. If you do too, fine. If you are not ready, gently let him know you appreciate the good discussion you just had, you are glad how well it went, yet you are not ready to make love. If you are ready at a later point, it would be really positive for you to mention it, rather than wait for him to raise it again.

APPENDIX 3

Men: Steps to Avoid Miscommunication

These steps are for men when they initiate the conversation. They are written with specific attention to the Female-ese aspects of communication.

1. Pick only one topic to discuss at a time. Be specific. Make sure you have her attention before you broach the need for a discussion. Do it during a quiet time, not while you are in the midst of an argument; not when she is doing laundry, fixing dinner or lunch for the kids, or otherwise occupied. Speak softly, without accusation or sarcasm. The purpose of this communication is to tell her you want to have a discussion on a particular topic.
2. Set an agreed upon time to meet. Be specific as to the day, hour, and location.
3. If you need a time frame, set the length of time to talk at whatever feels comfortable for you. (Women usually have a greater tolerance for these conversations.) One half hour to one hour is a reasonable time.
4. Come prepared, preferably having the issue you are concerned about in writing.
5. Practice what you want to say and how you want to say it. The purpose of this is to make sure you have

eliminated any accusations, included only I-Statements (no You-Statements). Practice keeping your voice at a low level but also expressing your feelings. Do not make this sound like a Board Meeting discussion.

6. Use I-Statements.

7. Avoid absolutes like "always," "never," and commands like "should," and "have/must/need to."

8. Repeat back what she has said to make sure you understood her point before you present your own point or take issue with hers. Do this for each of her statements. Have her do it for your statements.

9. If you are not absolutely clear what she means, ask her to explain: ask questions.

10. Stay focused on a solution that will help you avoid a similar problem next time. Do not bring up any past situations.

11. Do not be defensive.

12. Make sure you end with specific agreed upon suggestions for how to handle the situation this time and in the future. Write down what your agreement is so there will be no misunderstanding at some later point.

13. Make sure you end with a hug and/or a handshake.

14. Remember, you love each other. You are not enemy combatants; you are on the same team.

If you do this well, you will end up feeling more love and affection, knowing she has worked with you, not against you, to deal with an issue of great concern for you.

If you do this well, you may feel so close you want to make love with her. Caution: Make sure she wants to do it at that time also. She may need time to absorb what you have discussed. She may want to see if you are still affectionate (holding her hand, giving her a hug or kiss as you walk by, etc), that you don't just want to jump into bed. Bad timing on expressing your closeness, in Male-ese, can ruin a Good Argument.

Pick Your Battles Carefully

If you've been with a partner for a while, you probably have a number of complaints. It's rare for a couple to be so compatible that there are no areas of annoyance. Yet, you cannot be making constant attacks. You don't want your partner to pound you with a laundry list of complaints, so remember the golden rule: don't do this to your partner either. However, you don't want to avoid dealing with the issues either.

Therefore, you need a way to sort through your complaints. Most people are not even clear how many they have or how often they make them. (If you are brave, study yourself for a week, pen in hand. Track the number of times you complain about your spouse.) It's important to decide which complaints you can live with and which are not tolerable. Wise people pick their battles carefully.

Here are some guidelines for how to pick your battles.

1. Make a list of all your complaints about your partner. You may need a few days or weeks to gather them all.

2. Prioritize them — or at least categorize, i.e., (or "such as,") about how you are spoken to, about public behaviors, etc. Then prioritize within the categories.

3. As you look over your list, draw a line through those complaints you can live with if they never change. Challenge yourself to eliminate as many as possible, because the fewer complaints the better chance you have for success. Think in reverse: would you want your partner to hit you with a 25-must-change list? (You may want to reread Relationship Expectations.) Drop a complaint or keep it, but don't pretend to drop it yet quietly seethe about it.

4. Now that you have narrowed down the annoyances that have to be addressed, you need a system for doing so. You do not want to mention each complaint every time something offends you. Therefore, set a time once a week to discuss issues/complaints that arise during the past 7 days. This provides structure and removes what may feel like an ambush. It also allows you to let go of an annoyance more easily since you know you'll be getting back to it in a few days.

5. There will always be complaints, so the goal is not to remove them all, but to find a workable solution for the ones that you find intolerable.

6. Once you find a solution, write down what each of you agrees to do/not do when the situation occurs next. This should eliminate constant bickering about the same old things. ***A well-resolved issue doesn't keep reappearing.***

ALPHABETICAL INDEX OF WORDS

YOUR PERSONAL INVENTORY LIST

How to Use Your Personal Inventory List

Your Personal Inventory List is a tool for you and your partner (or you alone) to discover where gender differences may be getting you caught in repetitive conflicts or disappointments. Below is a list of all the words in the dictionary, with their subcategories. Using the male or female column put a check next to the words your recognize as problematic in your relationship. There may or may not be some overlaps in what you have each marked.

Using this list may help you narrow down the communication problems and understand your disappointment with your partner. You will see patterns in what may initally look like unrelated issues.

When you are in the midst of an argument (or later at a quiet time) come back to this list and reread the relevant words you have checked to see where you got tripped up. Discuss how each of you could have handled your own part differently, so you will be better prepared the next time the situation arises.

If you are doing this at a quiet time with your partner, you can reread the descriptions you each have marked and discuss how they show up in your arguments. (You can also do this by yourself, seeing where you missed the different Male-ese and Female-ese interpretations.

By recognizing how your misunderstandings of gender differences cause conflict, you can then create alternate responses when conflict arises. You can always have fun using the practice sessions from the Epilogue and Appendices.

The dictionary can continue to be an on-going resource for when ever a conversation or argument is not going well.

It is helpful if your partner does this with you, but not necessary. Since change only comes from chaning yourself, you can learn a lot and perhaps make a significant shift in your relationship just by your reacting differently – regardless what your partner says or does.

YOUR PERSONAL INVENTORY LIST

Male	Female	Page #	
			Advice
			Affairs
			Anger
			• Feeling of Anger
			• Action of Anger
			Apology/I'm Sorry
			Arguments
			• Meaning
			• Verbal Encounter
			• Stress and Physiology
			• Dirty Fighting
			• Tit for Tat
			• Deflect the Conversation
			• Good Argument
			Blame
			• Externalize
			• Internalize
			• Self-Blame
			• Personalize
			Change Yourself, Not Your Partner
			Communication Style
			• Verbal Tennis
			• Sharing Ideas

Male	Female	Page #

- Sharing Feelings
- Direct/Indirect
- Listening
- Voice Level

Competition

Compliments

Control
- I'm Right

Conversation
- Purpose
- Negotiation
- Questions
- Silence
- Nagging

Cultural Roles
- Men: If It Ain't Broke, Don't Fix-It
- Women: Prevent Problems from Becoming Bigger
- Problems with the Conflicting Roles

Emotional Pain

Fragile Ego

Gift Giving

I-Statements

I'm Fine

"I Love You"

Identity
- Core Identity
- Gender Characteristics

Male	Female	Page #

Intimacy
Last Word
Love/Hate
Mentor
Miscommunication
- The Miscommunication Cycle
- Question behind the Question

Name Calling
Never/Always/Should
Pleasing the Other
- Double Bind in Pleasing a Woman

Pronoun
QTIP
Relationship Expectations
- Shoebox and Mantel

Relaxation after Work
Sex
Pre-foreplay
- Female Aphrodisiac
- Kiss as Foreplay
- Intercourse
- Emotional Connection

Shame
Switching Shoes
Tears
Thank You

Male	Female	Page #

Time/Timing
- Timing in Arguments

We Have To Talk - About What?

Why Did You…?

Winner/Loser